THE DEER AND THE ANTELOPE
a meditation on law and disorder by Brenda Withers

Uproar Theatrics

LICENSING & PRODUCTION INQUIRIES
Uproar Theatrics, LLC.
hello@uproartheatrics.com I www.UproarTheatrics.com

CHARACTERS:
PAULIE, M (Late 20s/Early 30s), an ambitious realtor
JAMIE, F (30s), his equally ambitious boss
MEL, F (20s), their receptionist
KELLY/ LEA, F/F (20s), an optimistic new transplant to the
city / her heartbroken sister
RICHES, M (30-60), a gruff cop
BEEMB, M (30-60), his gruff partner

SETTING:
A contemporary American city. Now.

SYNOPSIS:
When a young woman is found murdered in a gentrifying
neighborhood, the search for suspects prompts a
disconnected community to question the roots of "random"
violence. A sideways glance at law-and-order, personal
responsibility, and the hidden costs of making a living.

LIGHTS UP on BEEMB, a detective, addressing the room. Maybe he has some visual aids accompanying his talk, or maybe the department cut that piece of the budget.

BEEMB

In 2019 we saw another marked decrease in city-wide crime, including a decline in the homicide rate, which fell from 4.5 per one hundred thousand citizens to 3.3 per one hundred thousand. This is in line with the continuous drop in the murder index we've seen over the last two decades, which we are happy to note reflects a dramatic abatement of over 65% since 1995 and one of the largest proportional major crime reductions the region has experienced since our department's incorporation.

I realize, of course, this is little consolation to the two hundred and eighty or so people for whom the murder rate in 2019 personally increased at a rate of approximately 100%, rising from a steady state of having never been murdered, having been murdered zero times their entire lives to now, having been completely murdered.

I don't want to get bogged down in statistics. The point is, things are generally better. For most of us. For now. Common, if unpopular, wisdom suggests that trends like this are cyclical, that any rate that's currently ebbing will eventually return to flow. Good policing requires we not take our eye off the ball just because it appears to have come to a rest. It's a ball. It's gonna roll again.

And when it does, we'll be there. We'll try to be there. There's a lot of there's here. But there's also a lot of police officers. We'll probably be there. Especially if it's outdoors, if it's happening outdoors, on the streets, public property, we have a very good chance of being there. And, fortunately, that's the area where crime rates tend to fluctuate: outside. Inside stuff— wives stabbing husbands, teenagers pawing MiMaw's jewelry— that stays fairly consistent, proportionally.

It's the incidents of quote-unquote-random violence, where assailants are unknown to their victims, that tend to rise in tandem with society's tensions. Mayhem amongst strangers increases as the number of strangers does, as the degree of the estrangement between those strangers does, as we pull further apart. Muggings, carjacks, identity theft— these are crimes motivated by cultural, not personal, frustration, pointing to an undercurrent of dissatisfaction between segregated populations. Unattended, these groups quietly transform themselves into more substantially defined opponents, engaging in a brand of intense, ongoing conflict often called, for want of a better term, war.

In the case of our city a class war, although we wouldn't go calling it that. Although that's what it will be. Although we wouldn't go calling it that. Maybe that seems foul or confusing, but it's not uncommon. In the midst of the Second World War, for instance, do you think people were walking around calling the Second World War "the Second World War"?

No. Does anyone— and they didn't call it World War Two— but does anyone know what they did call it? How that military action was commonly referred to, contemporarily?

Yeah, me neither.

That's because, as a nation, we don't really study our history anymore.
If we ever did. Which I can't speak to with certainty, as a non-history studier myself.

2

BEEMB (CONT)

I'm not proud of that, I'm just being honest. I'm not proud of it at all. Because it's people like me, and maybe you, the undereducated, the contently undereducated, who feed this cycle of ignorance and violence, who, after years and decades and generations of repeating "never again" stand always on the precipice of the next war-not-yet-named. Because when you don't learn your history, and when you don't learn from it, you're doomed to repeat it. You're doomed.

> *He holds his audience's gaze for a dramatic moment, then grabs his papers and dismisses them.*

Thank you, gentlemen.

> *LIGHTS OUT.*

> *LIGHTS UP on PAULIE, a real estate agent, and KELLY, a young woman. They sit across from each other in a well-appointed, windowless office.*

PAULIE

I. Am. Sorry.

KELLY

No!

PAULIE

I am *so* sorry. I thought for sure I'd be out in time.

KELLY

It's not a big deal—

PAULIE

I must have just missed you, too. I got out of the car, and I thought, I missed 'em. I missed 'em!

KELLY

It's okay. It's fine.

PAULIE

And then the first people I showed it to, took it.

KELLY

What?

PAULIE

First people. I told you, it's a nice place.

KELLY

Someone else took it?

PAULIE

But I have a million more. Don't worry about it.

KELLY

Uhhhh...oh.

PAULIE

Same neighborhood, same price range, same size. Bigger maybe.

KELLY

Same price?

PAULIE

Same price range, yeah.

KELLY

We. We really can't go any higher, I'm sorry, but—

PAULIE

If it's bigger?

KELLY

Sorry? Yeah, it's just, we don't really need bigger.

PAULIE

Everyone needs bigger.

KELLY

Uh. Huh, I, huh. Yeah, you know, we'd sacrifice bigger for cheaper.

PAULIE

Well, you'll sacrifice a lot for cheaper. This is a steal.

KELLY

I...I guess I just don't understand how the first one is gone.

PAULIE

It's like I said, it was an awesome place, first people who saw it took it. On the spot. Money down. Did you bring a check? Just in case we see something tonight—

KELLY

But weren't— sorry, but weren't we supposed to be the first ones to see it?

PAULIE

I know. I *just* missed you.

KELLY

But that wasn't our fault.

PAULIE *(unblinking)*

...It wasn't anyone's fault.

                    KELLY

It wasn't?

                    PAULIE

Nope. It's just. The city. Listen, don't worry about that one.
That one wasn't your place.

                    KELLY

But. You said it was. On the phone.

                    PAULIE

Hey. I hadn't met you yet, had I? Had I?

                    KELLY

No.

                    PAULIE

But now.

                    KELLY

Now you have my place.

                    PAULIE

Now I do.

            *He smiles. JAMIE, a supervising agent, pops her
            head in the door.*

                    JAMIE

How's it going in here?

                    PAULIE

Great.

                    JAMIE

Yeah?

6

PAULIE

Yeah.

JAMIE *(greeting KELLY)*

Hey, I'm Jamie.

KELLY

Hi.

PAULIE *(begrudgingly)*

Kelly, this is Jamie, another agent in the office.

JAMIE

I'm the supervising realtor.

KELLY

Oh. Nice to—

JAMIE

Where are you looking?

PAULIE

I'm taking her to Fulton. *(To KELLY)* You want to get going?

KELLY

Sure.

JAMIE

The two bedroom? For 28?

PAULIE

Yeah.

KELLY *(realizing)*

Oh, 2800?

JAMIE

The two bedroom on Fulton, right?

PAULIE

Off Fulton.

KELLY

Um, we actually talked about 2400?

PAULIE

Yeah, it's in range.

JAMIE

That's the one-bedroom. For twenty-four. Are you looking
for a spot for just you?

KELLY

Oh, no, there's—

PAULIE

There's a roommate.

KELLY

There's two of us, yeah.

JAMIE

Your boyfriend?

KELLY

Uhm—

JAMIE

Sorry! Girlfriend. Partner.

KELLY

Friend. Just friend from school.

JAMIE

Oh. In a one bedroom?

KELLY

I don't know, I guess.

JAMIE

You guys pretty close? Cause that'll be tight.

KELLY

That's. Whatever is the lower, the 2400, yeah, that'll be fine probably.

JAMIE

And that's a two year lease. On Fulton? Those are two years, so you want to be sure you have enough space.

KELLY

Yeah. We just want to be sure we can afford to pay the rent, though. Too.

JAMIE

Yes. Haha. Definitely. *(Smiles. Tension.)* Well, good luck!

KELLY

Thanks.

> *JAMIE leaves the office and KELLY and PAULIE continue to put on their jackets. As they're about to pop through the door, PAULIE signals for KELLY to wait—*

PAULIE

Actually, just one thing before we take off, okay? I gotta quick grab the—

And he's in JAMIE's office. KELLY sits out of earshot.

PAULIE

Jesus, Jamie.

JAMIE

What?

PAULIE

"What".

JAMIE

If you want to make your numbers this month, I'd throw them in the two.

PAULIE

I'm going to, Jamie.

JAMIE

That's what I would do.

PAULIE

They have to have enough, I have to figure out if they have enough for everything, security and first and fee, otherwise—

JAMIE

They have it.

PAULIE

Jamie.

JAMIE

They have parents, right? They have it.

PAULIE
All I'm saying is, I got it, okay? Just, when I'm in with a client—

JAMIE
I was trying to help! Sorry.

PAULIE
I know.

JAMIE
Everyone needs a little help sometimes, Paulie, it's not a personal attack.

PAULIE *(he disagrees, but)*
I know that, Jamie, and I appreciate it.

JAMIE
I remember you needing help before.

PAULIE
I've needed help on the numbers.

JAMIE
That's what I was trying to do.

PAULIE
I know.
...You don't know any other twos under 25?

JAMIE
Come on. Everything's up.

PAULIE
I know.

JAMIE

That's good, Paulie. That should make you smile, it's a good sign.

PAULIE

For us, I know, but for these kids—

JAMIE

They're not kids, they're not children.

PAULIE

They get money from their parents, Jesus, you just// said—

JAMIE

That's everyone now, that's the norm.

PAULIE *(After an audible sigh)*

Then is there...*(another audible sigh)*...

JAMIE

What.

PAULIE

Is there any way, I hate this, but is there any way, in terms of helping—

JAMIE

You want me to come with?

PAULIE

No.

JAMIE

I have a six-thirty, I can't come with tonight.

PAULIE

I don't— is there a way we can cut down the fee, reduce the
fee?

JAMIE smiles and shakes her head.

PAULIE

Not—

JAMIE

The broker's fee?

PAULIE

Yeah, but not by a lot.

JAMIE

You can reduce it by whatever you want, go ahead, reduce it.

PAULIE

Yeah, but—

JAMIE

But that comes out of your pocket. Not mine.

PAULIE

Jamie.

JAMIE

Paulie. I have to pay the rent here. I have to pay the rent on
this office.You want a desk? You want a light on your desk
and a printer and a coffee mug and coffee? You want a job?
It's a non-negotiable. The brokerage fee's non-negotiable.

PAULIE

Nothing's non-negotiable.

JAMIE

Everything's up.

LIGHTS OUT.

*LIGHTS UP on KELLY walking her
neighborhood, speaking into a cell phone.*

KELLY

Uhmmmm…no. No. No, Mom. Wait, say that again? No.

Mom, thank you, but no.
Because we don't need it.
Because it's the middle of November and we don't need an
air conditioner, in November you use heat.
Mom, of course the building has heat, it's a building!
I know. I know. I understand how seasons work, Mom, and
when it gets hot, in the summer, we will open the windows,
we have windows, we'll get a fan.
No. No! A window unit will take up all the light.
Yes, it will.
Yes, it will!
Don't send it. Don't send it. DON'T SEND IT, MOM.
Mom, seriously, even if you do, even if you do, we won't use
it.
We won't.
We won't put it in. It's not good for the environment.
Please don't compare fans to air conditioners, Mom.
Yes, it does too make a difference.
Uh, you're not a scientist.
Yeah, I know I'm not, I know that, we're *both* not scient—.
Mom. Mom. *Mom.*
*MOM, even if we wanted to put it in, we couldn't, okay, we
couldn't because there's bars on the window and it's not
going to fit an air conditioner!*

KELLY (CONT)

No, bars mean it *is* safe. That's what the bars are for, for safety.

It's fine. It's quiet, it's nice, it's very— Yes. Yes.

I know, but this is what we can afford right now. We *did* look there, we did, but *right now,* this is what we can—

Lots of people live here.

What does that mean, "kind of people"?

Well, I haven't met them all yet, I've only been here a week, so some of them are probably nice, some of them are probably not, some of them are probably poor. Like me. Yes, I

am. Yes,

I am.

I don't have money, so what would you call it?

(She smiles.) That's very creative. That's very funny.

I love you, too, Mom.

LIGHTS OUT.

LIGHTS UP on JAMIE's office, a few weeks later. Two detectives, RICHES and BEEMB, sit with JAMIE, waiting. It suddenly hits her she might offer them some…

JAMIE

Coffee? Do you guys want coffee?

RICHES

No, thanks.

JAMIE *(Standing)*

Let me get you some coffee.

RICHES

Nope. Thank you.

Beat. JAMIE is still standing.

JAMIE

Tea? Water?

BEEMB

You know, I'll take some coffee.

JAMIE

Oh, great. *(Off RICHES's slow burn look at BEEMB)* Now you want some, too, don't you? Now that he's having some.

RICHES

No.

JAMIE

Come onnn... *(Off RICHES's non-response)* I didn't make the coffee, if that's what you're worried about. Mel makes it. Did you guys meet Mel?

BEEMB

The girl at the front?

JAMIE

The girl at the front, yeah. Doesn't she look like she makes good coffee?

BEEMB	RICHES
Sure.	I don't know what that means.

RICHES *(Off BEEMB's look)*

I don't.

Small beat. JAMIE presses the intercom button on the desk.

JAMIE

Hey, Mel, can you bring a couple of coffees in here? *(To the detectives)* Regular? *(Off BEEMB's nod, back to the intercom)* Regular's fine, two regular coffees.

RICHES

I'm not gonna drink that.

JAMIE

Okay. Sure, okay, you don't have to.

RICHES

Right, and I'm not going to.

Beat. Beat.

JAMIE tries to act normally, as if she's able to go back to work with the two detectives sitting there. Maybe shuffles some papers, looks superficially over a form. The detectives stare silently at her.

RICHES

I had a bad experience with coffee once.

JAMIE *(looking up from her fake work)*

Hm? Seriously?

RICHES	BEEMB
Seriously.	No.

.

RICHES *(to BEEMB, off his intrusion)*

Yes.

> *Beat. RICHES looks at BEEMB. BEEMB looks at RICHES.*

JAMIE

Okay, well, we'll just get the one then, the—*(JAMIE presses the intercom)* Mel? Mel? *(Beat. MEL is not responding.)* Mel? I'll catch her in the kitchen.

> *And JAMIE's out the door. RICHES pokes around JAMIE's desk a bit.*

BEEMB

No warrant, Riches.

RICHES

Plain sight, *Beemb*.

> *Beat.*

BEEMB

What the hell were you talking about?

RICHES

What. When.

BEEMB

What are you talking about "bad experience with coffee"?

RICHES

Oh. Yeah, I tried it once—

BEEMB

Uh huh.

RICHES

And it tasted disgusting.

BEEMB

That's how coffee tastes.

RICHES

Well, for me that's a bad experience.

Beat.

BEEMB

We're homicide.

RICHES

Yeah.

BEEMB

You rank the taste of coffee as a bad experience next to
witnessing murders on a regular basis?

RICHES

I haven't witnessed that many actual murders. We usually
show up way after the fact. And also, I'm not the one getting
murdered. I *was* the one tasting the coffee.

*MEL appears in the doorway holding two cups
of coffee.*

MEL

Hi, excuse me, are these for you?

BEEMB   RICHES
Yeah.   No.

RICHES
Can I ask you something?

MEL

Okay.

RICHES *(holding out a crime scene photo)*
Have you ever seen this young woman?

> *At the sight of the photo, MEL gasps and drops the coffees.*
> *Quick BLACKOUT.*

> *Quick LIGHTS up on JAMIE, PAULIE, and RICHES gathered around the water cooler in PAULIE's office. RICHES has his foot propped up and is cleaning the bottom of his pant leg, inefficiently, with lots of water. BEEMB enters.*

BEEMB

She'll be fine.

RICHES

Yeah, *she* will.

> *He scrubs his pant leg.*

BEEMB

She just needs a second to collect herself.

JAMIE

I'm so sorry, she's usually very conscientious.

BEEMB

Sure. It happens.

20

RICHES

Yeah, around *coffee* it does.

BEEMB

Give it a rest, Riches.

RICHES

You give it a *rest*, the stain will set.

JAMIE

Yikes, is it a really expensive suit?

RICHES

Not anymore.

He scrubs.

PAULIE

You know, maybe I should go check on her, if she's upset?

BEEMB

Sure, that's a good idea. But how about if my partner takes
care of that, and we'll take care of this, and then we'll be out
of your hair, you go on with your day. Riches, you wanna go
look in on, uh, on our friend in the next room?

*RICHES stops scrubbing, huffily shakes out his
soaking wet pant leg, and heads next door.*

RICHES *(as he exits)*

Some friend.

Beat.

JAMIE

So.

BEEMB

So. You recognize her, right?

JAMIE

Yeah. I think. I didn't spend a lot of time with her, but Paulie
—

PAULIE

I didn't spend a lot of time with her either.

BEEMB

Right. How much?

PAULIE

Uhhh, couple hours. An hour. Couple.

BEEMB

Mmhm.

JAMIE

You're sure it's her?

BEEMB

Yeah, she still had her wallet on her, her license—

JAMIE

Oh that's good! *(Off BEEMB's look)* Just cause then you
could identify her. It's gotta be worse if you can't even say
who she is, if you can't pin that down.

BEEMB

Yeah. We pin it down.

JAMIE

Of course.

BEEMB

We have ways to get that information pretty quickly, most of the time.

PAULIE

Sure.

JAMIE

Most of the time, sure.

BEEMB

...Around all of the time.

JAMIE

Really? Wow, you—

BEEMB

The point here, Mr. Lagalos? *(To JAMIE)* Excuse me. *(Back to PAULIE)* The point here is that this is one of those times, one of those most of the times, where we do know who she is right off the bat, and *(To JAMIE again)* you're right, miss, that's cause she had her ID on her, and you're also right, that's a help. *(Back with PAULIE)* And in addition to her ID, she also had on her your telephone number. Mr. Lagalos. And so we're wondering if that's gonna be a help, too.

JAMIE

Absolutely.

A beat until PAULIE picks up on JAMIE's lead...

PAULIE

...Oh, *absolutely*, anything I can do to help, I'll help, I'm helping.

BEEMB

So you met the young lady where?

PAULIE

Here. Here, she, well, I *met-her*-met-her online.

BEEMB

Uh huh. Where?

PAULIE

Oh no, not— on craig's list.

BEEMB

Uh huh.

PAULIE

No, no, no. I'm a realtor.

BEEMB *(indicating the office)*

I'm aware.

PAULIE

I mean, that's why I'm on craig's list. The whole office is. We have to be.

JAMIE

I also occasionally sell furniture on there. My cousin owns a warehouse in Pennsylvania and I help him list overstock furniture. He pays tax, it's all— If that's important. *(BEEMB gives her nothing.)* It's probably not.

Beat.

BEEMB *(Back to PAULIE)*

You have emails?

PAULIE

Sorry?

BEEMB

You have an email record of your correspondence with Miss O'Heaney?

PAULIE

Uhhh...somewhere, yeah, yeah.

BEEMB

Is this your work computer?

PAULIE

Yeah...but, no. I do basically everything on my phone.

BEEMB

Okay, then we're gonna need to take a look at that.

PAULIE

Okay, but can I, could I just forward you the emails?

BEEMB

Yeah, you could. You could, but we'll still want to take a look. To make sure you forward us *all* of the emails.

PAULIE

Of course! Of course I will, I'm an honest guy.

BEEMB

Of course you are.

PAULIE

I mean, hey, I need my phone. To do my job.

BEEMB

That's a coincidence, I need your phone to do my job.

PAULIE *(Getting frustrated)*

Look, man, I just showed her apartments. This is a little—

BEEMB

You can call me, Sir.

PAULIE

Excuse me?

BEEMB

You can call me Sir. Or Officer, or Detective Beemb, or nothing. But do not call me "man".

PAULIE

Uh… okay.

BEEMB

Okay.

PAULIE *(Pushing back)*

Okay, and you can call me "Sir", too.

JAMIE

Paulie.

PAULIE

Since we're gonna get all formal here.

JAMIE

Paulie.

BEEMB

(To JAMIE, though with his eyes dead on PAULIE)

I think he'd like to be called, Sir. Ma'am.

PAULIE

Jesus Christ.

BEEMB

And *he* would definitely like to be called Sir.

JAMIE

Who?

PAULIE

Jesus Christ?

BEEMB

Sir Jesus Christ.

PAULIE

He's dead.

BEEMB

Not in my heart.

PAULIE

He was dead before people started using the word "Sir", way before people—

BEEMB

(cool but forceful, grabbing PAULIE by the lapels)
Not. In. My. HEART!!

JAMIE

(Freaking out, trying to break this up)
Oh God! Oh God! *(Realizing, amending, still freaking)* Oh *Sir* God, Oh *Sir* God! He's sorry! I'm sorry! Okay?! Okay? *(She looks out the open office door.)* Where's the other guy?

BEEMB

What other guy?

JAMIE

The other cop? *(Calling down the hallway)* Hello? The, the, the good cop!

BEEMB lets PAULIE free with a final shake.

BEEMB

I am the good cop. *(BEEMB heads for the door and calls over his shoulder)* I'll send CSU for your phone.

Beat. JAMIE and PAULIE look at each other in shock. They catch their breath. Then:

JAMIE

If you killed that fucking girl, you are fucking fired.

And JAMIE's out the door, too.

LIGHTS OUT.

LIGHTS UP on PAULIE's bedroom. PAULIE is doing some very particular nightly ritual, evening push-ups or something with skin creams. MEL sits comfortably in his bed, under the comforter.

MEL

But did you know you were putting her in a bad neighborhood?

PAULIE

What? No.

MEL

You didn't?

PAULIE

Well, what's a bad neighborhood?

MEL

Paulie.

PAULIE

What?

MEL

Come on, you know what a bad neighborhood is.

PAULIE

No, I don't. I don't, really. *(Off her look)* But you seem to, you seem to, so why don't you tell me?

MEL

Come *on*.

PAULIE

No, tell me what makes a neighborhood "bad".

MEL

Uhm, okay, maybe if it's a place where you might get murdered?

Beat. PAULIE seethes.

PAULIE

....Wow.

MEL

What?

PAULIE

That could happen anywhere, Mel.

MEL

No, it couldn't.

PAULIE

That could happen walking down the street anywhere,
anywhere in this country.

MEL

That's just not true, Paulie. You don't believe that.

PAULIE

It's absolutely true!

MEL

I don't believe that you believe that.

PAULIE

It doesn't matter what you believe! Logically, honestly,
people die *everywhere*. Does that make
everywhere a bad neighborhood? Are we living on a bad
entire planet?

MEL

But there are places you are more likely to die, where it
happens more often.

PAULIE

Like what, like your bed? Most people, I'd bet, I'd actually
bet you on this, without googling it, but I'd say *most people*
in the world, die in their own beds, have heart attacks or
strokes or whatever right there, at home.

MEL

Those people just *die*, Paulie, they're not *murdered!*

PAULIE

Neither was Kelly. You don't know she was murdered.

MEL

Yes, we do. The police came to see you!

PAULIE

That's right, the police came to see *me*, I'm the one who saw them, and the one who talked to them, and they didn't say murdered. They said she died.

MEL

They said she was killed.

PAULIE

That's not the same as murdered.

MEL

Yeah! Of course it is!

PAULIE

If it was the same as murdered, there wouldn't be a separate extra word, would there? We'd just say murdered, we'd just say murdered and leave it like that.

MEL

What?! Not—no, not true! Haven't you ever heard of, like, like, like synonyms?

PAULIE

Well, everyone's heard of them now, Mel, you're screeching like a hawk!

Beat.

31

MEL

Why did you call her Kelly?

PAULIE

What?

MEL

You just called her Kelly.

PAULIE

That's her name.

MEL

I know, but you said it like. *(A small beat.)* Are you sure you didn't know her?

PAULIE

Of course I knew her, I showed her// apartments, Mel, I—

MEL

No, are you sure you didn't know her, like, better? Like, a little better? She had your number in// her wallet.

PAULIE

I'm the one who told *you* that, Mel. *I* told *you* about her having my number in her wallet, okay, why would I do that if I thought it was some terrible secret? Like it's so incriminating, like it means anything other than what it means, which is that she was a hoarder, she didn't clean out her pockets and throw shit away like a normal person—

MEL

I don't think she was a// hoarder...

PAULIE

The point is, I didn't have to tell you anything.

MEL

Of course you did, the police came to see you!

PAULIE

And I could have just said that! The police came by, they
asked me some questions, they left. Case closed.

MEL

Not case closed, they took your phone.

PAULIE

Which I also didn't have to tell you about.

MEL

Well, then how would you have explained where the hell
your phone was?!

PAULIE

I wouldn't have explained it, I wouldn't have had to explain
it, Mel, because it's my phone. It's my phone, and my
business, and my life, and I don't have to tell every little
detail of it to my fucking receptionist!!

Beat.

MEL

I'm the office's receptionist.

PAULIE

Well, it's my office.

MEL

No, it's not.

PAULIE

It's more mine than yours.

MEL

Wow. Wow. Congratulations.

A long moment. Then finally...

PAULIE

We had one drink.

MEL

What? *(She takes this in, and takes it hard. Perhaps a little too hard.)* Oh no.

PAULIE

Nothing happened, Mel. I took her for a drink because we were waiting on a landlord and I felt bad that I'd rented another apartment she wanted, so I bought her *one* drink. And then we went to the appointment. And that was it.

MEL

...What kind of a drink?

PAULIE

What?

MEL

What kind of a drink did you buy her?

PAULIE

I don't know. A midori sour.

MEL

Oh *no*. What kind of drink did you have?

PAULIE

Oh my god, will you stop?

MEL

What does this mean?

PAULIE

Nothing.

MEL

No, if it meant nothing, you would have told me, right? She had your number in her wallet, it means nothing, you tell me. But you didn't tell me about the drink—

PAULIE

It's—

MEL

You probably didn't tell the police about it either.

PAULIE

There's nothing to tell, Mel.

MEL *(a conscious shift)*

…Okay.

PAULIE

Okay?

MEL

Yeah.

> Beat. PAULIE gets into bed. MEL lays quietly
> for a moment, trying to hide the shift in her
> thinking. Then…

MEL

…I'm really thirsty.

PAULIE

What?

MEL gets out of bed. She's wearing pajamas and is barefoot.

MEL

I'm gonna, I'm gonna go get something to—

PAULIE

You have a glass of water right there.

MEL

I want something else, I want juice.

MEL has made her way to a nearby chair over which most of her clothes are splayed. As unobtrusively as possible, she attempts to slip on her high heeled booties and grab her coat, her bag, her clothes. She can't get it all before PAULIE catches on.

PAULIE

You just brushed your teeth.

MEL *(More nervous)*

It's okay, it's okay, I'll brush them // again—

PAULIE

What are you doing?

MEL

Nothing. I don't feel // well—

PAULIE

Mel.

Feeling the gig is up, MEL gives up on
retrieving any more items and makes a break
from the bedroom. It's clumsy and quick, she's
got her bag, a sweater, and her shoes half on.
He coat remains. PAULIE starts out of bed.

PAULIE

Melanie!

MEL *(From the other room, with real terror in her voice)*
Just leave me alone. Leave me alone!

And we hear the front door to the apartment
open and slam shut. PAULIE stands there for a
moment in shock. Eventually he makes his way
to the window to look down on where she's gone.

LIGHTS OUT.

LIGHTS UP on a vigil. LEA, a woman who
looks a lot like KELLY, stands at a makeshift
podium and speaks to a crowd of people holding
lit candles, flowers, signs with KELLY's face on
them. She reads, kind of dramatically, from a
small notebook, perhaps into a bullhorn.

LEA

If you really want people to know who you are,
If you want people to really know who are,
If you want people to know who you really are,
get murdered.

If you just die, people will be interested, especially if you're
young or pretty and especially if it's sudden. But their

interest won't be in you, it'll be in death, mortality, fate. They'll put your name in the middle of sentences, they'll frame your face on a funeral home easel, but what they'll really be focusing on is themselves. "It could have been me, it could have been me, it could have been me".

But if you get murdered, killed, a team of professionals will be dispatched to your door, with pocket-sized notepads and paper shoes. They'll walk gently from room to room, or if you live in a studio apartment from side of room to side of room, they'll run their gloved fingers over your dusty windowsills, through the leftover curry containers in your fridge, deep into the pockets of your jeans. They will use cameras and satellites and the DMV to pinpoint your most recent whereabouts, purchases, heartbreaks. They will read your diary. If you don't keep one of those, your emails. If you don't keep one of those, your fingerprints or the worry lines on your face or what's left of it.

They will study you like the mystery you are and have always been. And they may not find your killer, but there are more important things in life than blame.

LEA stops reading and speaks off the cuff.

My little sister wrote this six weeks before she died. I found it in a journal that was given to me by the police after they did all those things she said they would do. To some, it probably seems a little magical that Kelly maybe predicted her own fate. But it makes sense to me and everyone who knew her, because Kelly was, in many ways, magical. She had a magical smile and magical eyes and a magical laugh. She could also stop time. And fly. She was a witch. I'm making jokes because, um, because I feel so bad. My parents feel so bad. They, they haven't—

LEA breaks down quietly and stops speaking. She stands there for a long moment trying to compose herself. She does not let the crowd really see her cry.

LEA (CONT)

We think she was attacked around 2 AM last Saturday at the entrance to the Smith Street subway station. If you were there at that time or know anyone who was or think you have any information that might be useful to the investigation, please, please, please contact the police. I loved my sister so much. And she was right when she said there is something more important than blame. There's revenge.

The crowd offers some stunned, sporadic applause. Maybe a few start to sing a weird protest song, something at once appropriate and the opposite, like something similar to an a cappella version of "Empire State of Mind" or "We Built This City". LEA takes this in. She hates and is grateful for it at the same time.

LIGHTS OUT.

LIGHTS UP on JAMIE on a machine at the gym where a dance mix of whatever song was being sung at the vigil is now being played in the background. She is watching TV and dominating whatever piece of gym equipment she's chosen, maybe a stationary bike. She speaks to the person on the machine next to her, a little too loudly, about a story that's on the television.

JAMIE *(a gasp)*
I know her! Yeah! She's a client, she was a client! Awful!
Scary!

> *She shakes her head as if to say "Awful/ Scary"*
> *at once.*

So sad!

> *She makes a so-sad face. Over the course of this*
> *next section her eyes fix back on the TV before*
> *her, and she talks probably more to herself than*
> *her neighbor, possibly in a weird mash-up of*
> *linear thought and workout-motivational-*
> *speech. This is not strange for JAMIE.*

It makes you pretty anxious, to be close to someone like that.
I mean, some people it makes them anxious to be close to
anyone, and then add on top of that if that someone is a
disappeared person, a dead person? A victim? I almost just
stayed home this morning instead of coming here, I almost
just stayed home and made blueberry muffins. And ate them!
Ate, them, up! But then these are the times when you really
have to stay on your game. You have to keep respecting your
body, keep investing in your most important property, keep
keep keep what you have have have! Unless you have
gingivitis, like my cousin, and then that you have to get rid
of.

Like, if the house next to yours got robbed, would you fling
open all your windows and turn off your alarms? No way, *no*
way— you'd turn them up! Up, up, up! Keep, it, tight! Your
castle, your rules! Your crown, your jewels! Your—

(Interrupting her own chant) It's called personal
responsibility! Which is the cornerstone of community

JAMIE (CONT)

responsibility, when you think about it, when you think about it, what do they say on an airplane? Put your mask on first! You have to be able to breathe through your weird plastic bag before you help anyone else breathe through theirs. Even kids! Even little kids. It's funny, but in some ways, putting other people second, is actually putting other people first! Yeah. If your seatbelt isn't on, it's not just dangerous for you, it's dangerous for everyone near you, if you go flying out of your seat you'll break everybody else's nose, I don't care what you weigh.

(Realizing that her last statement could be taken out of context at a gym she checks in again with her neighbor.) I don't. Muscle weighs more than fat. That's a fact. I'm not a nutritionist, but.

She smiles at her neighbor. She keeps exercising.
LIGHTS OUT.

LIGHTS UP on the police station. BEEMB and RICHES are working, organizing papers and stapling piles of them together. BEEMB runs out of staples.

BEEMB

You have any staples?

RICHES

Nope.

RICHES staples another pile of papers. BEEMB
Seriously?

RICHES

Just the ones in here.

> *BEEMB looks around his desk for an extra box of staples in vain, as RICHES continues to staple his papers. Until RICHES runs out as well. He takes a moment before...*

RICHES

Hm. You have any?

> *Beat during which BEEMB just looks at him.*

BEEMB

Why would I ask you for staples if I had some?

RICHES

So you don't?

BEEMB

Why wouldn't I just use my own?

RICHES

I don't know. Maybe you're stingy.

> *Beat.*

BEEMB

Thanks.

> *Beat.*

RICHES

I said maybe.

*Instead of getting up to find staples in some
other part of the police station, RICHES tries to
affix the papers before him through alternative
means. He hits them very hard and quickly with
his hand, perhaps. BEEMB watches at least one
of these failures unfold. He considers his
partner.*

BEEMB
…When did you take the detective's test?

RICHES

Sorry?

BEEMB

What was your score?

RICHES

Confidential.

BEEMB

Did you pass the first time?

RICHES

That's *confidential.*

*BEEMB rises with his stapler and leaves the
room.*

RICHES *(calling after him)*
If you're headed to get you-know-what I could use a box,
too!

*Instead of moving on to another performable
task, RICHES stays focused on his papers and
doesn't notice MEL entering at first. When he*

*looks up, he sees she's been crying and maybe is
still. She clutches her oversized bag tightly.*

                    RICHES

Oh boy.

          *From her bag MEL produces a few personal
          items and places them on RICHES's desk: a
          hairbrush, a dirty glass, and a sweater.*

                    RICHES

What's all this?

                    MEL

It's, it's, it's—

                    RICHES

You wanna sit down?

          MEL *(speeding through to prevent a crying jag)*
We, we had a fight, but I went back to his apartment—

                    RICHES

Whose?

                    MEL

What?

                    RICHES

Whose apartment?

                    MEL

Mr. Lagalos. Paulie.

                    RICHES
You call him, // Mr. Lagalos?

MEL

I went back when he was supposed to be at work to get this stuff, but he wasn't at work and we had another fight, but I managed to grab some of this and I brought it, I brought it to you, I don't care what happens, it's the right thing to do.

RICHES

…You want some water?

MEL

No.

RICHES

Notice I didn't say coffee?

MEL

I'm sorry.

RICHES

Cause coffee can cause a lot of problems in a workplace.

MEL *(crying)*

I'm sorry, I'm sorry! I said I was sorry yesterday!

RICHES

I remember.

MEL

But, I mean, I've never seen anybody dead before—

RICHES

That's alright.

MEL

No, it's not, I don't want to see dead people. You shouldn't have shown me a dead person.

RICHES

Ma'am.

MEL

How would you like it? What am I talking about, you'd probably love it, that's why you chose your job, so you could get to see things like that all the time. But I didn't, I chose to be something else, I chose something where I would basically *never* see a dead person—

RICHES

You chose to be a receptionist.

MEL

Yes.

RICHES

You chose to be a receptionist at a real estate broker's office.

MEL

Yes! Well, no, I didn't *choose* to be *that*, I'm, I'm not *that*, my job. I have a lot more going on—

RICHES

Obviously. Hey, Ma'am? *(She shakes her head, doesn't answer.)* Ma'am? I have some good news for you, okay? You ready for some really good news?

MEL

Yes.

RICHES

We didn't show you a dead person.

MEL

...What?

RICHES

That dead person you were so upset over seeing? You didn't
see it.

MEL

I...what?! That wasn't a dead person?! H—

RICHES

Of course not. Of course not, Ma'am. *(Beat.)* That was a
picture of a dead person.

MEL

.....

RICHES

That was just a photograph. The dead person wasn't with us,
we can't carry a dead person around with us while we do our
questioning. We drive a sedan. The dead person's in the
morgue.

MEL

What?!

RICHES

That can't be a surprise to you.

MEL

A surprise to me, a surprise to me is the way you're speaking
right now!

RICHES

My accent?

MEL

No!

                    RICHES
I'm from Indiana.

                     MEL
You're, you're, you're making jokes! You're—

                    RICHES
At a time like this.

                     MEL
Exactly!

                    RICHES
I'm just trying to make you feel better, Ma'am. I'm trying to
calm you down a little because I've found a calm witness is
always better than a crying one.

                     MEL
I'm a witness?

                    RICHES
You tell me.

                     MEL
No.
I mean, no, I would tell you, but no, I don't know what to
say. I don't know what I should say.

                    RICHES
Say the truth.

                     MEL
I don't really know what the truth is.

                    RICHES
Yeah, join the club. The philosophy club. It's down the hall.

MEL

What?

RICHES

You do too know what the truth is. You do, too. You came
here with something on your mind.
Something in your bag.

*RICHES eyes the items on his desk. MEL
explains.*

MEL

I brought it. For DNA.

RICHES

Okay.

MEL

I thought you could test it. If you think Paulie's— if you
need to test it.

RICHES

Mmhm. You know we have kind of official procedures for
that. For the ways we collect evidence.

MEL

Oh. Oh, so you can't use it?

RICHES

I didn't say that. *(He considers the items, maybe moves them
around with a pencil so as to avoid leaving prints.)* What
size is this sweater?

MEL

It's— what?

RICHES

Detectives don't make that much. I'm not proud.

MEL

It's a woman's sweater.

RICHES

I'm not proud.

MEL

I'm— it's not mine. It was in his apartment and it's not mine.
I thought, could it maybe have been hers? The, the, the
victim's?

RICHES

Hm.

MEL

I'm not trying to get him in trouble.

RICHES

Oh, clearly.

MEL

I'm just really confused. Like, see something, say
something, right, but— *(she starts crying again.)*

RICHES

No! No.

MEL

I can't help it.

RICHES

No, listen, there's nothing to be upset about. You're doing
the right thing.

                         MEL
Not for Paulie.

                        RICHES
You're doing the right thing for someone more important
than Paulie, for someone who died.

                         MEL
But I don't feel like I'm doing the right thing.

                        RICHES
Well, imagine how the dead person feels.

Unless that's gonna start you crying again, then just imagine
something else, imagine a warm breeze on a warm night.

Everyone always says cool breeze in that scenario, cool
breeze on a warm night, but I think that's disjointed, I don't
find that settling at all. I'm the kind of person'd rather
imagine outfits that match, you know? Red shoes with a red
skirt, red lipstick, and all the same red, balloon.

Imagine basketball teams where all the players are the same
height, and so are all the players on the opposing team, so
are all their speeds and talent levels, so are their haircuts.
Maybe their hearts beat different, maybe they're driven
internally by different stuff— fame, family, a secret drug
addiction, but we can't see that, we're sitting here on evenly
laid out bleachers, lines of unknotted wood running parallel
to each other in a gymnasium lit by a hundred hundred watt
light bulbs all shining at max. We're comfortably packed
next to people with legs the same length as ours, sharing
cartons of popcorn flavored with the same flavored salt we
all like best. We all know what time it is, we all know the
score, we all agree with every call the refs have made, no
one in the whole arena has an early morning tomorrow. And
more than we're cheering for one team or the other to win,

the blue or the green, the bad boys or the reigning champs,
we're cheering in blissful, medium-volumed unity for this
perfectly paired, plain-too-fair game to mercifully, finally
end.

LIGHTS OUT.

*LIGHTS UP on PAULIE in a bar. He speaks to a
captive audience, guy or girl, doesn't matter, we
don't see them. We do see that PAULIE is on his
way to drunk.*

PAULIE

So then I was like, 'Yeah, but you think everything is your
fault.'
And she was like, 'I do think that.' She does think that. That's
her whole problem!
She should have thanked me, for pointing it out. Some
people it takes them their whole lives to zero in like that. But
instead she goes, "And you think nothing is."
Meaning 'nothing is your fault', my fault, meaning I think
nothing is my fault.

I don't think that! I don't think that.

I *know* some things are my fault, okay? Okay?
My credit score? Okay.
Myyyy….posture.
Certain car accidents.
One time I gave a dog back to the animal shelter, even
though I knew he'd be, you know, put down if I did, this cool
little black schnauzer. But I did it, and he was. I said I
brought him back because I turned out to be allergic, but
really it was just that walking him took up so much time and

PAULIE (CONT)

I wanted to be able to go to the gym in the evenings instead.
More consistently. So that was on me.

Sorry, is this too much?
(Without really waiting for an answer) It's just like, what is
she actually accusing me of? Did I kill the girl by letting her
rent an apartment in a shit part of town or did I kill her with
my bare fucking hands?
Maybe both!
No, no, no. Maybe *neither*.
It's neither, it's neither, relax.

Like, where does it end?
If I eat a hamburger, did I kill a cow? No.
Yes. But not alone, not on my own, not in a world where
everyone's on board with hamburger eating, where there are
like a million hamburger eaters, a billion— how many
people are there are on the planet? But then how many of
them are vegetarians?
And how many of those vegetarians are like *really*
vegetarians, you know? My friend Lila is a vegetarian, but
she eats salmon, I don't understand that.

My point is…my point is… why is it on me? What about us?
What about those other thirty people who ate from that same
cow, ate steaks, ate, used bones for mulch or for soup or
whatever, tacos. Fajitas. *(He dives deep into this list,
meaning each example, perhaps getting freer and more
vulnerable as they progress.)* Chimichangas. Chalupas.
Carne Asada. Beef nachos.
   *(He begins to sing, sweetly, sincerely, the only Latin-
influenced song he thinks he knows.)* Guantanamera. Guarija,
Guantanamera. Guan-tan-a-meeeee-ra. *(He sings and dances
   for a while. He is making a scene, but it's very authentic.)*
   I'm just trying to live my life! Like everyone else. I'm just
alive!

*LIGHTS UP on BEEMB looking over a wall
display in JAMIE's office. We hear the sound of
phones ringing, everywhere. Maybe the phone in
JAMIE's office starts to ring, then stops. Then
starts again. Then stops and a light on it just
blinks incessantly. JAMIE enters, harried.*

JAMIE

Sorry! So sorry.

BEEMB

No, no.

JAMIE

It's been crazy, it has been crazy here.

BEEMB

I can see.

JAMIE

It's like, I can't answer every call in this place. I can't even
answer every *phone* in this place, I didn't even know we had
this many phones.

BEEMB

Lot of phones.

JAMIE

Our receptionist hasn't been in. Mel, the girl, um, you met
her, I think.

BEEMB

Yep.

                    JAMIE
I don't know what's up with her, if she's—.
You'd think she'd at least have the decency to call in sick.
Call in with some excuse.

                    BEEMB
Maybe she did.

                    JAMIE
What?

                    BEEMB
        (indicating the blinking light on the phone)
Maybe that's her right now.

                    JAMIE
Oh. Oh, I doubt it.

                    BEEMB
Me, too.

        Beat.

                    JAMIE
So. Paulie isn't here. My colleague.

                    BEEMB
I can see that.

                    JAMIE
I don't know where he is. Either. He hasn't been in for three
days. If that matters.

                    BEEMB
Matters to you, I bet.

JAMIE

Yeah. Yes, definitely, but I mean, I don't know if you're looking for him or something. He's not here.

BEEMB

Right.
(With some unnecessary cop-gravity) Well, I am looking for him. I am here for him.

JAMIE

Oh god. *(She sits.)* Oh my god.
I can't believe it.

(A big gasp.)
And I *can* believe it, you know? Wow.
What an idiot.

BEEMB

Who?

JAMIE

I thought he was, I thought he was—
He has keys to my apartments! He has keys to all my apartments.
The office's apartments, the—Shit.
How do I get those back? Do you keep all his stuff?
Do you take all his stuff into custody?

BEEMB

Do we take all his stuff into custody?

JAMIE

Yeah. Please don't stonewall me here, I know you have to
be official and everything, but I need to get those keys back.
I have to protect my clients.
And myself.
And my clients. They could be in danger. *(She searches his
face for a hint.)* Are they in danger?

BEEMB

No more than usual.
I came to return Mr. Lagalos's personal items.

JAMIE

Oh my god, he's dead?!

BEEMB

Not that I know of.

JAMIE

Thank god. Maybe I shouldn't care if he was, I know, if he's
a murderer, but I'm not like that, I'm just not like that. I
believe in the sanctity of all life.

BEEMB

Terrific.

JAMIE

I wish we could all live forever.

Beat.

BEEMB

I'm understanding he's not here at the moment, but if you do
think Mr. Lagalos will be returning at any point in the future,
or if Ms. Chiffel will, it would be a help if we could leave
these here for them to sort out.

JAMIE

Ms. Chiffel, like Melanie?

BEEMB

She brought these to us at the precinct, but said they were his, and we don't have the means to get to the bottom of whether that's true, who owns what. We don't really want to get into a whole thing.

JAMIE

You don't have the means?

BEEMB

Um…we don't have the motivation. Mr. Lagalos is no longer of interest to the investigation.

JAMIE

He's— *(She sits again. This means she stood sometime earlier.)* You just, you just told me he killed her!

BEEMB

I did not. I didn't.

JAMIE

You let me believe it!

BEEMB

Uhhi let people believe whatever they want. It's a free // country.

JAMIE

I almost fired him!

BEEMB

How can you fire someone who's not working for you?

JAMIE

What?

BEEMB

Hasn't been here for three days, you said. Sounds like maybe he quit.

JAMIE

S…ts…ts…maybe he has the flu!

BEEMB

Maybe.

JAMIE

He would never quit on me. He loves this job.

BEEMB

Okay, ma'am.

JAMIE

He makes bank at this job.

BEEMB

Okay.

JAMIE

Makes more than you do.

BEEMB

Probably not.

JAMIE

Probably!

BEEMB

…Probably not, ma'am.

Beat.

                          JAMIE
You're sure it wasn't him?

                          BEEMB
Pretty much. Security camera caught some footage of the
victim talking to a homeless couple a few days in a row, we
followed that up and looks like it was a pretty
straightforward money grab. One guy got aggressive. She
resisted. He resisted that resistance. Head, cement, then the
rest.

                          JAMIE
Oh my god, they hit her with cement?

                          BEEMB
She—
The sidewalk.

                          JAMIE
Oh. Ohhh. Wow.
Okay, well, I'll let Paulie know. If he ever shows his face.

                          BEEMB
Yeah, and I don't want to tell you how to run your business,
but you may want to also let your clients know.

                          JAMIE
About Paulie?

                          BEEMB
About the incident. The neighborhood.

                          JAMIE
But you got the guy, right? Who did it?

BEEMB

We did, we do.

JAMIE

So, it's not like an unsolved, whatever, mystery.

BEEMB

No, not a mystery.
But it might be a, uh, we like to watch for and consider the
possibility of trends. Citywide. As precaution, you know?

JAMIE *(She doesn't)*

Mmmm.

BEEMB

Prices go up, neighborhoods change, there's gonna be
resentment.

JAMIE

I know.

BEEMB

Gonna be—

JAMIE

Jealousy, I know.

BEEMB

…Desperation. There's gonna be more than one desperate
homeless person out there.

JAMIE

Yeah. *(Indicating the still blinking light on the phone)* That's
probably some of them right now!

BEEMB

….

JAMIE
(Rolling up her sleeves to get back to work)
Gotta keep doing our part, right? Keep contributing
somehow.

BEEMB
Yeah. Somehow.

LIGHTS OUT.

*LIGHTS UP on PAULIE sitting across a table
from LEA in a cafe. A long quiet as they take
each other in. Finally...*

PAULIE
So thanks. Thank you for meeting with me.

LEA
Sure.

PAULIE
I know you're still going through...everything. Still. With
your family.

LEA
....

PAULIE
I wanted— I felt like I needed to let you know that, My life
has really changed. I've changed it.
A lot.

LEA
.......Oh.

PAULIE

I quit my job. I broke up with my girlfriend.

LEA

Oh.
Because of my sister?

PAULIE

No. Although, *yes*, actually—

LEA

I'm sorry, are you saying that you two—

PAULIE

No, no, no. No, no, // no.

LEA

Okay, cause—

PAULIE

We were just— no, we were nothing.
Not nothing. I'm trying to be more conscious with my words.
(He thinks for a moment.) We were acquainted.
Professionally.
And personally, but that's my business, the professional is personal in my business. Was. We weren't, uh, romantic— not that we couldn't have been, she was very pretty.

LEA

…Thank you.

PAULIE

Like you.
She looked a lot like you. You look like her. Right?

                              LEA

Yes. Thank you.

                             PAULIE

I'm not hitting on you.

                              LEA

Thank you.

          Beat.

                             PAULIE

Full disclosure, my girlfriend actually broke up with me.
Full disclosure, she wasn't my girlfriend, she was my
secretary. She was my secretary *and* my superior's secretary.
We shared her. Not like that.

                              LEA

Did she know my sister?

                             PAULIE

No.

          Beat.

                             PAULIE

You know how out of something really bad something good
can come?

                              LEA

No.

                             PAULIE

Oh.
It can.

LEA

Okay.

PAULIE

And, like, in this instance, the really bad— the, you losing
your sister—

LEA

I didn't lose her.

PAULIE

What?

LEA

She's not lost.
She's dead.

PAULIE

Yeah.

> *Beat.*

PAULIE *(continuing deliberately, but a little spooked)*
Yeah, so, but
Out Of That
I Learned

I don't know if you know this, but I was accused, basically,
I was almost accused of being somehow involved in the
situation? And, I wasn't, I wasn't,
but
I was.

I put her in that apartment.
I showed her that apartment in that neighborhood, and then I
told her she'd love it.

PAULIE (CONT)

I was lying.
Not exactly, cause I can't tell the future, and I didn't know
her that well, but my guess? My hunch? She wouldn't love
it. She wouldn't even like it.

But I didn't care, because I was even, I think I was even a
little bit mad at her for not taking this other apartment, this
other more expensive one that she said she couldn't afford,
but I thought she could, I thought she could have somehow,
could've called her parents—

LEA

She could have.
She should have.

PAULIE

I was blinded, by by by, what's it—self worth.
No, self interest.
I can't blame my job entirely for that, but I do blame it
somewhat. Everybody in that industry is...It's just a reality:
my job was partially responsible for me being partially
responsible for your sister's death.

LEA

.....

PAULIE

And that's why I quit.

LEA

.....

PAULIE

.....

LEA

What are you gonna do now?

PAULIE

Oh, I got another job. It's a non-profit, so.
I help sell carbon off-sets, do you know what those are? It's
like, when you take a plane somewhere you create a lot of
pollution, the fuel, but if you pay extra money, we'll plant
trees to offset that, to make it disappear.

LEA

I know what they are.

PAULIE

It's pretty cool. I feel good about it.
I feel like, in some ways, I'm offsetting, it's an offset, like a
job-offset, like I did a bad job for a long time and now I can
make up for that by doing a good job. I did a good job at a
bad job, now I'm gonna do a great job at a good job.
I mean, I'm still working on commission, which I know is
not perfect—

LEA

It's— why's that?

PAULIE

What?

LEA

What's wrong with working on commission?

PAULIE

Oh, cause
It's a system based in, you know, corporate— capital— it's
more is more.
More is more, no matter the, the, the consequence.

LEA

Well,
the consequence is
More.

PAULIE

Exactly, and more and more
and more and
more.

LEA

And what's wrong with that?

PAULIE

It never stops.

LEA

…And what's wrong with that?

Beat.

LEA

You left your job because you didn't like making money?

PAULIE

Um.

LEA

Or you didn't like that you liked making money?

My sister was like that. She had a big heart. Open mind.
She recycled and ate organic and talked to people.
Homeless people and
People selling things for non-profits
Which I imagine are often cross-over populations, I bet there
are a lot of people who graduate from selling trees to living
in the subway.

PAULIE

I don't sell the trees.

LEA

My sister was killed by a poor person, you understand that?

PAULIE

I know.
I heard.

LEA

Not someone interested in commission. Not someone interested in money.

PAULIE

Oh, but, okay, I'm not trying to argue with you here,
Didn't the guy who,
Wasn't she robbed?
So wasn't he? Interested in money?

LEA

Uh, okay, he wasn't interested in *real* money, consistent money, in *working* for money. He wasn't interested in earning it, he didn't think it ought to cost him anything.

PAULIE

It, it cost him a lot. He's in jail.

LEA

It cost *me* a lot. It cost my parents a lot. It cost Kelly.

PAULIE

Yeah. No, yeah.

LEA

That guy's thrilled to be in jail. He has a bed now. He has a place to live.

PAULIE

Right.

LEA

You should have tried to make a commission on that. You should rent out jail cells to homeless people, you'd clean up.

Beat.

LEA

I, um, have to go.

PAULIE

Sure, okay.

LEA

Um, can we get the—
Or I'll just leave you cash for it, five, six?

PAULIE

No, no, no. I got this.

LEA

No, you don't need to buy me a // latte.

PAULIE

                                                                    I got it.

LEA

You don't have a job.

PAULIE

I do.

LEA

You don't have a good job.

PAULIE

I'd like to get it.

LEA

No thank you.

PAULIE

I'd like to get it.

LEA *(letting go)*

I'd like to be a fucking giant fucking movie star, alright?!
Doesn't mean I should, doesn't mean it's a smart, reasonable
thing for me to pursue.

My sister was completely irresponsible! She was not stupid,
she was not new, she was stubborn. She refused to see the
world for what it is.
You think her dying is some big wake up call for your life?
Fine! Wake up!
You not making money doesn't mean other people won't,
doesn't mean they'll stop wanting to, suddenly! You're not
that influential, you're not gonna destroy human greed or
undo anyone's instincts, you're not that good a salesman!
You'll just be one more disappointed do-gooder pretending
not to be disappointed and you'll end up just like her.
Or just like the people who hurt her.
Broke, broken. Dangerous.
That's not honoring her life
That's honoring her death
And I don't want to do that.

PAULIE

…I don't want to do that either.

Long beat.

71

PAULIE

Can I just say one thing?

LEA

….

PAULIE

I think you actually could be a giant fucking movie star.

LEA

Stop.

PAULIE

If you really wanted. I told you, I already said, you're very pretty.

LEA

…You *are* hitting on me.

PAULIE

You wish.

They share a smile.

PAULIE

You know, your sister didn't wanna let me buy her drink either.

LEA

…What?

PAULIE

We were out
Once
We were waiting on an appointment
And, uh, anyway, I wanted to get it and she put up a big fight.

LEA

Oh. Yeah?

PAULIE

Yeah. Just like you.

LEA

...Worse things I could be like than my sister.

PAULIE

Definitely.
I mean, I did eventually convince her. I'm a better salesman than you think.

LEA is not totally successful at resisting a smile.
LIGHTS OUT.

LIGHTS UP on MEL and RICHES across from each other at a desk in the police station. MEL reads from a notepad and holds a pen to make changes. RICHES paces the room, listening.

MEL

"The department would like to thank the community for their remarkable outpouring of help, without which we would not have made such...", etc, etc.

She presents, with equal dispassion, the second option.

"The department would like to thank the community for *its* remarkable outpouring of help, without which we would not have made such...", etc.

                    RICHES
Hm. Hm.
What's the difference?

                    MEL
"Its" / "Their".

                    RICHES
What. Where.

                    MEL
No, "it's". Versus. "Their".

                    RICHES
Their what?

                    MEL
Detective Riches.

                    RICHES
Police Administrative Aide Trainee Chiffel.

                    MEL
It's Chiff-el.

                    RICHES
What's the difference.

          MEL *(Done, but still professional)*
Okay, I think you're all set here, I think this is a very good
speech as is.

                    RICHES
Nn. What about the third paragraph?

MEL

What about it?

RICHES

Do you think it belongs?

MEL

I don't know what that means. It's your press conference,
can't you say anything you want? I think as long as you give
the speech with confidence and it's mostly facts—

RICHES

Oh, I'm not giving it.
I'm not giving it, Beemb is.
I have terrible stage fright.

MEL

You—
It's not a play.

RICHES

Not yet. Could be. Could become one, it's a really interesting
story. And I don't want to be represented as a nervous person
in that instance, I don't want to go down in history as a
coward.

MEL

…Okay.
Okay, then I'm gonna just type it up then.

RICHES

Use a big font, he has small eyes.

MEL

…..

MEL turns to a desktop computer and starts

typing. RICHES doesn't leave.

RICHES
Who do you think would play you?

MEL
Hm?

RICHES
In the play. If this became—

MEL
I don't—

RICHES
Don't be humble, don't be shy, who do you think would
really be the best person, honest opinion, the best
professional actor, stage actor, okay, to portray you? In the
adaptation.

MEL
I—

RICHES
And then who do you think would be me?

MEL
I don't think it would make a very good play.

*Silence. Except for her continued typing.
Eventually:*

RICHES
What?

MEL
It's not funny.

76

RICHES

So? Most plays are sad.

MEL

It's not really sad either.

RICHES (*a scoff*)
Yeah? Then why'd you cry so much?

MEL

What? I did//n't.

RICHES

Come on, you been waterworks basically every step of the
way.

MEL

I have not, I haven't cried once since I started working here,
I've been very professional, I— I'm not crying now.

RICHES

Yeah, cause now it's over.

MEL

No, it's not. It's not.
We're still talking about it, we're still writing about it, you're
gonna give a speech about it—

RICHES

Beemb is giving the speech.

MEL

That girl is still dead. And she'll be dead forever. That
doesn't end. That guy who killed her still did it. He's still a
murderer.
Paulie still isn't. I'm still someone who thought he was. I'm

MEL (CONT)
still someone who thinks he is, sometimes.
When I wake up, if the room is dark, or before I put my
contacts in, sometimes I do still think that.
That doesn't feel done to me.

She types.

RICHES
Well, police work isn't about feelings, it's about facts, Police
Administrative Aide Trainee. You're gonna have to get a
handle on that.

MEL
Oh, I agree. I agree, it's the facts that are giving me the most
trouble. They don't add up.

RICHES
Yes, they do.

MEL
Not to a number I… feel comfortable with. Like, did you
ever read—

RICHES
Siddhartha?

MEL
Um, no.

RICHES
Valley of the Dolls. Jurassic Park.

MEL
…Okay, *I, I* used to read a lot of books by, um, Agatha
Christie, like whodunits? I was in this library club where
whoever read the most would win a prize, like a bike I think.

RICHES

Bike's not a good prize for a library club, bikes don't make you wanna read.

MEL

Yeah.

RICHES

Prize should have been more books. Or glasses.

MEL

But so, uh huh, I read all these Agatha Christies because you can get through them pretty quick. And they were always really good, really British and detailed and— but then you'd get to like the last chapter, and the guy who did it was, like, out of nowhere. Some character you'd never even heard of, a gardener or uncle or something—

RICHES

Butler.

MEL

Exactly, lots of butlers, just somebody who had no connection up til that point to the rest of the book, and then, boom, he's the killer, he's the cause, he's the problem.

RICHES

Well, that's how it happens sometimes.

MEL

No, I know, obviously, it's just— You don't want to read that book. You don't want to see that play. It doesn't make you feel… settled or smart or like, like, like your life holds together, it doesn't make you feel like things are connected—

RICHES

Okay, here we are with the feelings again.

MEL

Sorry.

RICHES

You don't *feel* butlers are connected to their bosses, the houseguests, the people they kill with the candlestick? You think muggings and murders are random if it's not between two people who went to high school together? That's feelings. That's feelings getting in the way of facts. Again. I mean, how old were you when you were reading these books? Twenty? In your twenties? MEL
I'm in my twenties now.

RICHES

Okay, nineteen?

MEL

I wasn't in a library club when // I was nineteen.

RICHES

My point is, you're a little more sophisticated now, right? You have a more nuanced sense of perception. Just cause you didn't see the connection then, doesn't mean it wasn't there. So, same with now. You don't know everything yet. You can't see the whole map. If there's a streetlight's busted over an alley, doesn't mean the alley isn't there, doesn't mean it won't get you from A to B, as fast, faster than the bright, beautiful, familiar boulevard running parallel. You want things to add up, you want connection, you want closure, okay— don't deny the alley; fix the streetlamp. Talk to the butler. Maybe give him a raise. Before he grabs the candlestick.

MEL looks at RICHES.

She types a little, her eyes still on him.

RICHES

Don't put that last part in the speech, Beemb's father was a candlestick. I mean a butler.

LIGHTS OUT.

Lights up on BEEMB at a podium. He reads the speech RICHES prepared, as if it is his own.

BEEMB

And finally we want to thank the community for their remarkable outpouring of help, without which we may not have made such steadfast and significant progress towards this investigation's conclusion. When we suggest our citizens should say something, if they see something, this is what and why and how and where and...what...we're talking about. Your sense of service and vigilance and morbid curiosity spurred dozens of potential leads in this case, most of which, of course, turned out to be irrelevant or redundant or suspiciously motivated, and none of which actually led to the apprehension of the suspects we currently have in custody— But!— *all* of which still. Made. A difference. You kept our tip line operators very busy, and— you may not know this, it's a little inside baseball, but— the more calls our operators log in, the easier it is for us to get our CrimeStoppers budget passed by the city council, and that's not nothing. To the contrary, it's about $73,000 a year. Is that enough money to stop crime? Probably not. But does that mean we shouldn't spend it? Does that mean we shouldn't try?

BEEMB (CONT)

A few years ago my wife had a dinner party where she served an appetizer of potato florentine puffs. They're pastries with potatoes and spinach and they're very good. People ate them all night long, long past the end of the appetizer course, after dessert even. Before we retired to the living room for charades, I noticed that one of our guests had a little bit of green stuck in his tooth. I didn't want to embarrass him— or myself— by mentioning it directly, so I just said, to the whole table, "Hey everybody, don't forget to check those chompers for chow!" It was cute. All the people with clean teeth ran their tongues over their gums. The man who had the spinach stuck in there did nothing. He just laughed at what he thought was my joke, mouth open, tooth green.

What went wrong? I'd seen something, I'd said something, and Carl didn't listen. Why couldn't he have been more receptive to me? Why couldn't I have been more direct with him? Why couldn't my wife have served something that better matched the color of our teeth: cauliflower, french bread, a nice bowl of milk pudding? There are lots of culprits here. Lots of people and circumstances and recipes from the internet to hold responsible.

I don't know if blame games work. This department has been playing them for a long time and I can't really say if we're winning. We've got a lot of people in uniform, we've got a lot of people in jail, but is that what victory looks like in the realm of modern criminal justice: dress blues and orange jumpsuits? Personally, I'd prefer an empty prison to a packed one. I'd prefer a world where we don't have to call the cops on each other because we're committed, in any small way, to policing our own behavior, beating ourselves to the punishment. I'd like to pick up a call on the tip line and hear a voice telling me all they saw today was courtesy and kindness. I'd like to hear someone say the something they saw was themselves in the mirror, their own greedy heart, great mistakes, green teeth. But don't worry: they got it, they cleaned it, it's fixed, and we can end shift early. We can all go home now. We can all go home.

LIGHTS. END OF PLAY.